When Life Hurts

Understanding God's Place in Your Pain

PHILIP YANCEY

Multnomah® Publishers *Sisters, Oregon*

WHEN LIFE HURTS
published by Multnomah Publishers, Inc.

© 1999 by Philip Yancey and SCCF
International Standard Book Number: 1-57673-673-3

Cover photograph by Adobe Image Library
Design by Christopher Gilbert

Scripture quotations are from
The Holy Bible, New International Version
© 1973, 1984 by International Bible Society,
used by permission of Zondervan Publishing House

Multnomah is a trademark of Multnomah Publishers, Inc.,
and is registered in the U.S. Patent and Trademark Office.
The colophon is a trademark of Multnomah Publishers, Inc.

Printed in the United States of America

For information:
MULTNOMAH PUBLISHERS, INC.
POST OFFICE BOX 1720
SISTERS, OREGON 97759

Library of Congress Cataloging-in-Publication Data

Yancy, Philip
    When life hurts: understanding God's place in your pain/by Philip Yancey.
      p.   cm.
    ISBN 1-576-73673-3 (alk. paper)
    1. Pain–Religious aspects–Christianity. 2. Suffering–Religious aspects–Christianity
    3. Consolation. I. Title

BV4909.Y36 1999
248.8'6 21—dc21   99-045664

99 00 01 02 03 04 05 — 10 9 8 7 6 5 4 3 2 1

When my heart was grieved
and my spirit embittered,
I was senseless and ignorant;
I was a brute beast before you.

Yet I am always with you;
you hold me by my right hand.
You guide me with your counsel,
and afterward you will take me into glory.

Whom have I in heaven but you?
And earth has nothing I desire besides you.
My flesh and my heart may fail,
but God is the strength of my heart
and my portion forever.

Psalm 73:21-26

Introduction

I n three decades of writing, I've talked to many people in pain. Some of them, like one teenage pilot who ran out of fuel and crashed in a cornfield, were directly responsible for their own suffering. Others, like a young woman who died of leukemia six months after her wedding day, were seemingly struck at random, with no warning. Yet all of them, without exception, experienced deep and nagging doubts about God because of the pain.

Pain calls our most basic beliefs about God into question. Over and over again I have heard five major questions brought on by pain. Is God competent? Is he really so powerful? Is he fair? Why doesn't he seem to care about pain? And, where is God when I need him most?

I know those questions well, for I have also asked them when I have suffered. If you have not yet asked them yourself, you probably will someday, when

severe pain or heartache strikes. If you are caught in a web of suffering, whether physical or emotional, this little book is for you. In these most unwelcome times of searching and despair, God longs to give us something beyond value, something we never asked for. Each question can become an invitation to hope, the doorway to his gracious gifts.

All my longings lie open
before you, O Lord:
my sighing is not
hidden from you. My
heart pounds, my
strength fails me;
even the light has gone
from my eyes.

Psalm 38.9, 10

SECTION ONE

When you wonder why God created pain.

Take a walk in a garden in the springtime or watch snow fall on a mountain landscape, and for a moment all seems right with the world. Creation reflects God's greatness as a painting reflects the genius of an artist.

The world abounds with beauty, to be sure.

But look closer at this lovely world and you begin to notice pain and suffering everywhere. Animals devour each other in a vicious survival cycle of eat and be eaten. All humans endure deep personal sorrows. Some of us destroy one another. Everything that lives confronts blight, accident, or disease—and eventually dies.

God's "painting" appears flawed, at times even ruined.

I confess that I once viewed pain as God's one great goof in an otherwise impressive world. Why would he mess up such a world by including pain in it? Without injury and suffering, we would find it so much easier to respect and trust him. Why didn't he create all the beautiful things in the world, but leave out pain?

I discovered the answer to this question in an unusual place. To my amazement I found that a world without pain actually exists—within the walls of a leprosy hospital. People with leprosy, today called Hansen's disease, do not feel physical pain. But as it turns out, that is the peculiar tragedy of their condition. As the disease spreads, nerve endings that carry pain signals fall silent. Virtually all the physical deformity comes about because the leprosy victim *cannot* feel pain.

I once met a leprosy patient who lost all the toes on his right foot because he insisted on wearing tight and narrow shoes. I know another who nearly lost his thumb because of a sore that developed when he gripped a mop handle too hard. Scores of patients at that hospital have gone blind because leprosy silenced the pain cells designed to alert them when to blink.

"Pain is not an innovation God devised at the last moment of creation just to make our lives miserable."

My encounters with leprosy victims showed me that in a thousand ways large and small, pain serves us each day. If we are healthy, pain cells alert us when to change shoes, when to loosen our grip on a mop handle or rake, when to blink. In short, pain allows us to lead a free and active life. In a previous book, *Where Is God When It Hurts*, I described some of the remarkable features of the pain network in our bodies. I cannot reproduce them all here, but a few are worth mentioning:

Without pain's warnings, most sports would be far too risky.

Without pain, there would be no sex, for sexual pleasure is mostly carried by pain cells.

Without pain, art and culture would be very limited. Musicians, dancers, painters, and sculptors all rely on the body's sensitivity to pain and pressure. A guitarist, for example, must be able to feel exactly where his finger lands on the string and how hard it presses.

Without pain, our lives would be in constant

mortal danger. We would have no warning of a ruptured appendix, heart attack, or brain tumor.

In short, pain is essential to preserve normal life on this planet. It is not an innovation God devised at the last moment of creation just to make our lives miserable. Nor is it his one great goof. I now look at the incredible network of millions of pain sensors all over our bodies, precisely gauged to our need for protection, and see an example of God's competence, not incompetence.

Without pain, our lives would be in constant mortal danger.

O my God, I cry

out by day, but you

do not answer.

-Psalm 22:2

SECTION TWO

When you doubt God's power.

Of course physical pain is only the top layer of what we call suffering. Death, diseases, earthquakes, tornadoes—all of these summon up hard questions about God's involvement on earth. It is one thing to say he originally designed pain as an effective warning for us. But what about the world now?

Can God possibly be satisfied with all the rampant human evil and natural disasters and child-killing diseases? Why doesn't he step in with all his competence and put an end to some of the worst kinds of suffering? Is he powerful enough? Does he have the ability to rearrange the universe in a way that would relieve our suffering?

A famous philosopher once posed the problem of pain this way: "Either God is all-powerful or all-loving. He cannot be both and allow pain and suffering." This line of thinking has often led to the conclusion that God is good, loves us, and hates to see us suffer; but unfortunately, his hands are tied. He simply isn't powerful enough to straighten out the problems of this world.

But this is not what the Bible teaches. Turn to that Old Testament book about a man who suffered great, undeserved pain. With Job, God had a perfect platform to discuss his lack of power, if that indeed was the problem. Surely Job would have welcomed these words from God: "Job, I'm truly sorry about what's happening. I hope you realize I had nothing to do with the way things have turned out. I wish I could help, Job, but I really can't."

God said no such thing. Speaking to a wounded, thoroughly demoralized man, he celebrated his own wisdom and power (Job 38-41).

"Brace yourself like a man," God began. "I will question you, and you shall answer me." Then God launched into a tour of the cosmos. "Where were you when I laid the earth's foundation? Tell me, if you understand. Who marked off its dimensions? Surely you know!"

Step by step, God led Job through the process of creation: designing the planet earth, carving out troughs for the sea, setting the solar system into motion, working out the crystalline structure of snowflakes. Then he turned to animals, pointing with pride to the mountain goat and the wild ox and ostrich and horse and hawk. Writer Frederick Buechner summed up the confrontation in Job in this way: "[God] says that to try to explain the kind of things Job wants explained would be like trying to explain Einstein to a little-neck clam.... God doesn't reveal his grand design. He reveals himself."

Other parts of the Bible convince me that perhaps we ought to view the problem of pain as a matter of timing, not of power. We get plenty of indication that God is dissatisfied with the state of this world, surely as dissatisfied as we are. And one day he plans to do something about it.

All through the prophets and through Jesus' life

and the New Testament runs a theme of hope, of a great day when a new heaven and new earth will be fashioned to replace the old. The apostle Paul puts it this way, "I consider that our present

sufferings are not worth comparing with the glory that will be revealed in us. The creation waits in eager expectation for the sons of God to be revealed. . . . We know that the whole creation has been groaning as in the pains of childbirth right up to the present time" (Romans 8:18–19, 22).

At times, living in this "groaning" creation, we cannot help feeling like poor old Job, who scratched his sores with shards of pottery and wondered why God was allowing him to suffer. Like Job, we are called to trust God, even when all the evidence seems stacked against us. We are asked to believe that he does control the universe and that he plans a much better world someday, a world without pain or evil or heartache.

Like Job, we are called to trust God, even when all the evidence seems stacked against us.

How long,

O Lord?

Will you forget

me forever?

How long will you

hide your face

from me?

Psalm 13:1

SECTION THREE

When God seems unfair.

W

"hy me?" we ask almost instinctively when we face great tragedy.

Look at these questions carefully and you can detect a common thread.

Two thousand cars were driving in the rain on the expressway— why did mine skid into a bridge?

Out of all the kids that go to school why was my son shot by a madman?

A rare type of cancer strikes only one in a hundred people—why did my father have to be among the victims?

Each questioner assumes that God was somehow responsible, that he directly caused the pain. If, in fact, he is all-competent and all-powerful, then doesn't that mean he controls every detail of life? Did God personally select which car would fishtail across the highway? Did he direct the gunman to his victim? Did he choose a cancer victim at random, out of a telephone book?

Few of us can avoid such thoughts when pain hits us. Immediately we begin to search our consciences for some sin that God must be punishing: *What is God trying to tell me through my pain?* And if we find nothing definite, we begin to question God's fairness. Why am I suffering more than my neighbor, who is an outright jerk?

The suffering people I have interviewed torment themselves with such questions. As they writhe in bed, they wonder about God. Often, well-meaning Christians only make them feel worse. They come to the hospital room bearing gifts of guilt ("You must have done something to deserve this") and frustration ("You must not be praying hard enough").

"To be commanded to love God at all, let alone in the wilderness, is like being commanded to be well when we are sick, to sing for joy when we are dying of thirst, to run when our legs are broken. But this is the first and great commandment nonetheless. Even in the wilderness—especially in the wilderness—you shall love him."

Frederick Buechner

Once again, the only place to truly test out our doubts about God is the Bible. What do we find there—does God ever use pain as punishment? Yes, he does. The Bible records many examples, especially of punishment directed against the Old Testament nation of Israel. But notice: in every case, punishment follows repeated warnings against the behavior that merits the punishment. The books of the Old Testament prophets, hundreds of pages long, give a loud and eloquent warning to Israel to turn from sin before judgment.

Think of a parent who punishes a young child. It would do little good for that parent to sneak up at odd times during a day and hit the child without any explanation. Such tactics would produce a neurotic, not an obedient, child. Effective punishment must be clearly related to behavior.

The nation of Israel knew why they were being punished; the prophets had warned them in excruciating detail.

The pharaoh of Egypt knew exactly why the ten plagues were unleashed against his land: God had predicted them and told him why they would happen and how a change of heart could prevent them.

Biblical examples of suffering-as-punishment, then, tend to fit a pattern. The pain comes after much warning, and no one sits around afterward asking, "Why?" They know very well why they are suffering.

But does that pattern resemble what happens to most of us today? Do we get a direct revelation from God warning us of a coming catastrophe? Does personal suffering come packaged with a clear explanation from God? If not, I have to question whether the pains most of us feel—a skiing accident, cancer in the family, a traffic mishap—really are punishments from God.

Frankly, I believe that unless God specially reveals otherwise, we would be best to look to other biblical examples of people who suffered. And the Bible contains some stories of people who suffered but definitely were not being punished by God.

"I do not believe that sheer suffering teaches. If suffering alone taught, all the world would be wise, since everyone suffers. To suffering must be added mourning, understanding, patience, love, openness, and the willingness to remain vulnerable."

Anne Morrow Lindbergh

Jesus made this point at two different places in the New Testament. Once, his disciples pointed to a blind man and asked who had sinned to bring on such suffering—the blind man or his parents. Jesus replied that neither one had sinned (John 9:1-5).

Another time, Jesus commented on two current events from his day: the collapse of a tower that killed eighteen people and a government-ordered slaughter of some worshipers in the temple. Those people, said Jesus, were no guiltier than anyone else (Luke 13:1-5). They too had done nothing to deserve their pain.

There are exceptions, of course. Some pain does have a clear connection to behavior: victims of venereal disease and smoking- and alcohol-related illnesses don't need to waste time trying to figure out the "message" of their pain.

However, most of us, most of the time, are not being punished by God. Rather, our suffering fits the pattern of unexpected, unexplained pain such as that experienced by Job and the victims of the catastrophes Jesus described.

The Lord is righteous in all
his ways and loving toward
all he has made.

Psalm 145:17

Record my lament; list
my tears on your
scroll—are they not
in your record?

Psalm 56:8

SECTION FOUR

IV

When you wonder if God cares.

The last great doubt that arises in the midst of pain is subtly different. This one is personal. Why doesn't God show more concern for us in a time of need? If he cares about my pain, why doesn't he let me know it?

A great Christian author named C. S. Lewis wrote a classic book on pain, called simply *The Problem of Pain*. In it, he answered convincingly many of the doubts that spring up when Christians suffer. Hundreds of thousands of people have found comfort in Lewis's book.

But years after Lewis wrote the book, his wife contracted cancer. He watched her wither away in a hospital bed and then watched her die. After her death, he wrote another book on pain, this one far more personal and emotional. And in that book, *A Grief Observed*, C. S. Lewis says this:

> Meanwhile, where is God? This is one of the most disquieting symptoms. When you are happy, so happy that you have no sense of needing Him, if you turn to Him then with praise, you will be wel

comed with open arms. But go to Him when your need is desperate, when all other help is vain and what do you find? A door slammed in your face, and a sound of bolting and double bolting on the inside. After that silence. You may as well turn away.

C. S. Lewis did not question the existence of God, but he did question God's love. At no time had God seemed more distant or unconcerned. Did God really love? If so, where was he at such a time of grief?

Not everyone feels the sense of abandonment described by C. S. Lewis. Some Christians express that God became particularly real to them in their time of grief. He can offer a mysterious comfort that helps transcend the pain we are feeling. But not always. Sometimes he seems utterly silent. What then? Does God care only for people who somehow feel his comfort?

I have talked to enough people in pain to realize that experiences differ. I cannot generalize about how any individual will experience the closeness or distance of God. But there are two expressions of God's concern that apply to all of us, everywhere. One is the response of Jesus to pain. And the other involves everyone who calls himself a Christian.

Even the most faithful Christians may, like C. S. Lewis, question God's personal concern. At such a time, prayers seem like words hurled into the void. Few of us get a miraculous appearance of a loving God to calm our doubts. But at least we have this: an actual glimpse of how God truly feels about pain.

He was despised and rejected by men, a man of sorrows, and familiar with suffering.

Isaiah 53:3

Jesus spent much of his life among suffering people, and his response to them also shows us how God feels about pain. When Jesus' friend died, he wept. Very often—and every time he was directly asked—he healed the pain.

How does God feel about our pain? Look at Jesus. He responded to hurting people with sadness and grief. And then he reached out with supernatural power and healed the causes of pain. I doubt that Jesus' disciples tormented themselves with questions like "Does God care?" They had visible evidence of his concern every day. They simply looked at Jesus' face, and watched him as he performed God's mission on earth.

In Jesus we have the historical fact of how God responded to pain on earth. He gives the up-close and personal side of God's response to human suffering. All our doubts about God and suffering should, in fact, be filtered through what we know about Jesus.

*In his life on earth,
Jesus endured far
more pain than most
of us ever will.*

Not only did Jesus respond with compassion to pain, the amazing fact is that God himself took on pain. The same God who boasted to Job of his power in creating the world chose to subject himself to that world and all of its natural laws, including pain. Another Christian writer, Dorothy Sayers, put it this way:

> For whatever reason God chose to make man as he is—limited and suffering and subject to sorrows and death—He had the honesty and courage to take His own medicine. Whatever game He is playing with His creation, He has kept His own rules and played fair. He can exact nothing from man that He has not exacted from Himself. He has Himself gone through the whole of human experience, from the trivial irritations of family life and the cramping restrictions of hard work and lack of money to the worst horrors of pain and humiliation, defeat, despair, and death. When He was a man, He played the man. He was born in

poverty and died in disgrace and thought it well worthwhile.

"For God so loved the world," says the Bible's most familiar verse, "that he gave his one and only son, that whoever believes in him shall not perish but have eternal life" (John 3:16).

The fact that Jesus came and suffered and died does not remove pain from our lives. Nor does it guarantee that we will always feel comforted. But it does show that God did not sit idly by and watch us suffer alone. He joined us and in his life on earth endured far more pain than most of us ever will. In doing so, he won a victory that will make possible a future world without pain.

*The word "compassion" comes
from two Latin words that mean "to
suffer with." Jesus showed compassion in
the deepest sense when he voluntarily
came to earth and took on pain.
He suffered with us,
and for us.*

Show the wonder of your great love, you who save by your right hand those who take refuge in you.... Keep me as the apple of your eye; hide me in the shadow of your wings.

Psalm 17:7-8

SECTION FIVE

When you need to feel God's love.

But Jesus, our suffering Savior and healer, did not stay on earth. Today, we cannot fly to Jerusalem, rent a car, and schedule a personal appointment with him. How can we sense God's love in a tangible way today?

We have the Holy Spirit, of course, an actual sign of God's presence in us. And we have the promise of the future when God will set the world right and meet us face to face. But what about right now? What can reassure us physically and visibly of God's love on earth?

That is where the church comes in, the community that includes every person on earth who truly follows God. The Bible uses the phrase "the body of Christ," and that phrase expresses what we are to be about.

Christians are called to represent what Christ is like—his words, his touch, his care—especially to those in need.

There is only one good way to understand how the body of Christ can minister to a suffering person, and that is to see it in action. I have seen it and experienced it in my own life. And I have seen it working in the life of others. Let me tell you about Martha, a person who lived with great pain and great doubts.

Martha was an attractive twenty-six-year-old woman when I first met her. But her life was permanently changed one day when she learned she had contracted ALS, or Lou Gehrig's disease. ALS destroys nerve control. It first attacks voluntary movements, such as control over arms and legs, then hands and feet. It progresses until finally it affects breathing, causing death. Sometimes a person's body succumbs quickly, sometimes not.

Martha seemed perfectly normal when she first told me about her illness. But a month later she was using a wheelchair. She got fired from her job at a university library. Within another month, Martha had lost use of her right arm. Soon she lost use of her other arm and could barely move the hand controls on a new electric wheelchair.

I began visiting Martha at her rehabilitation hospital. I took her for short rides in her wheelchair and in my car. I learned about the indignity of her suffering. She needed help with every move: getting dressed, arranging her head on the pillow, cleaning her bedpan. When she cried, someone else had to wipe her tears and hold a tissue to her nose. Her body was in utter revolt against her will. It would not obey any of her commands.

We talked about death and, briefly, about the Christian faith. I confess to you readily that the great Christian hopes of eternal life, ultimate healing, and resurrection sounded hollow and frail and thin as smoke when held up to someone like Martha. She wanted not angel wings, but an arm that did not flop to the side, a mouth that did not drool, and lungs that would not collapse on her. I confess that eternity, even a pain-free eternity, seemed to have a strange irrelevance to the suffering Martha felt.

She thought about God, of course, but she could

hardly think of him with love. She held out against any deathbed conversion, insisting that, as she put it, she would only turn to God out of love and not out of fear. And how could she love a God who let her suffer so?

It became clear around October that ALS would complete its horrible cycle quickly in Martha. She had great difficulty breathing. Because of reduced oxygen supply to her brain, she tended to fall asleep in the middle of conversations. Sometimes at night she would awake in a panic, with a sensation like choking, and be unable to call for help.

Martha's final request was to spend at least two weeks out of the hospital in her own apartment in Chicago. She saw this as a time to invite friends over, one by one, in order to say goodbye and to come to terms with her death. But the two weeks in her apartment posed a problem. How could she get the round-the-clock care she needed? Government aid could be found to keep her in a hospital room, but not at home, not the intensive care she needed just to stay alive.

Then a group of Christians stepped forward to offer the free and loving personal care that Martha needed. They adopted Martha as a project and volunteered all that was necessary to fulfill her last wishes. Sixteen women rearranged their lives for her. They divided into work teams, traded off baby-sitting duties for their own children, and moved in. They stayed with Martha, listened to her ravings and complaints, bathed her, helped her sit up, moved her, stayed up with her all night, prayed for her, and loved her. They were available. They gave her a place, and gave meaning to her suffering.

To Martha they became God's Body. The women also explained to Martha the Christian hope. And finally, Martha, seeing the love of God enfleshed in his body, the people around her—although to her God himself seemed uncompassionate, even cruel—came to that God in Christ and presented herself in trust to the one who had died for her. She did not come to God in fear; she had found his love at last. Finally, on the faces of those Christian women

"Do not let your hearts be troubled.
Trust in God; trust also in me.
In my Father's house
are many rooms; if it were not
so, I would have told you.
I am going there to prepare
a place for you. And if I go and
prepare a place for you, I will
come back and take you to be
with me that you also may
be where I am.

John 14:1-3

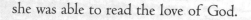

she was able to read the love of God.

In a very moving service in Evanston, she feebly gave a testimony and was baptized.

On the day before Thanksgiving, Martha died. Her body, crumpled, misshapen, atrophied, was a pathetic imitation of its former beauty. When it finally stopped functioning, Martha left it.

Today Martha lives, in a new body, in wholeness and triumph. She lives because of the victory that Christ won over pain and sin and suffering and death. And she discovered that victory because Christ's body, the church, made it physically known to her. Through her suffering, she learned what he was truly like. In the love and compassion of the Christians around her, she saw and received the love of God himself.

And her doubts about him gradually fell away.

The apostle Paul must have had something like that process in mind when he wrote these words:

God comforts us in all our troubles, so that we

can comfort those in any trouble with the comfort
we ourselves have received from God. For just
as the sufferings of Christ flow over into our
lives, so also through Christ our comfort overflows.

2 Corinthians 1:5

The best answers to the questions raised when life
hurts are found in Christ's body, the church. By minister-
ing to those who suffer, we let God's comfort overflow
through us. In doing so, we let the world know what God
is really like.

"If we love God and love others in Him, we will be glad to let suffering destroy anything in us that God is pleased to let it destroy, because we know that all it destroys is unimportant. We will prefer to let the accidental trash of life be consumed by suffering in order that His glory may come out clean in everything we do."

Thomas Merton